NATIONAL GEOGRAPHIC | **GLOBAL ISSUES**

HUMAN
RIGHTS

Andrew J. Milson, Ph.D.
Content Consultant
University of Texas at Arlington

Acknowledgments

Grateful acknowledgment is given to the authors, artists, photographers, museums, publishers, and agents for permission to reprint copyrighted material. Every effort has been made to secure the appropriate permission. If any omissions have been made or if corrections are required, please contact the Publisher.

Instructional Consultant: Christopher Johnson, Evanston, Illinois

Teacher Reviewer: Patricia Lewis, Humble Middle School, Humble, Texas

Photographic Credits

Front Cover, Inside Front Cover, Title Page ©Murat Taner/Corbis. **4** (bg) ©Peter Turnley/Corbis. **6** (bg) ©EPA/SERGEY DOLZHENKO/Newscom. **8** (bg) Mapping Specialists. **10** (bg) ©Robert Madden/ National Geographic Stock. **12** (br) ©Miraflores/epa/ Corbis. **13** (bg) ©AP Photo/Fernando Llano. **14** (bg) ©Chico Sanchez/EPA/Newscom. **16** (bg) ©REUTERS/Crack Palinggi. **18** (tr) ©Hulton-Deutsch Collection/Corbis. **19** (bg) ©Jacques Langevin/Sygma/Corbis. **20** (bg) ©Mast Irham/EPA/ Newscom. **22** (bg) ©John Bul Dau. **23** (tl) ©Scott Peterson/Getty Images. **24** (bg) ©NORMAN NG KRT/Newscom. **27** (t) ©MARK RALSTON/AFP/ Getty Images/Newscom. **28** (tr) ©Pascal Povani/ AFP Creative/Getty Images. **30** (tr) ©NORMAN NG KRT/Newscom. (br) ©Patrick Robert/Corbis. **31** (bg) ©Martin Benik/Westend61/Corbis. (tr) ©Per-Andre Hoffmann/LOOK/Getty Images. (br) ©Pascal Povani/AFP Creative/Getty Images.

MetaMetrics® and the MetaMetrics logo and tagline are trademarks of MetaMetrics, Inc., and are registered in the United States and abroad. The trademarks and names of other companies and products mentioned herein are the property of their respective owners. Copyright © 2010 MetaMetrics, Inc. All rights reserved.

For permission to use material from this text or product, submit all requests online at www.cengage.com/permissions

Further permissions questions can be emailed to permissionrequest@cengage.com

Visit National Geographic Learning online at www.NGSP.com.

Visit our corporate website at www.cengage.com.

Printed in the USA.

RR Donnelley, Menasha, WI

ISBN: 978-07362-97936

13 14 15 16 17 18 19 20 21 22

10 9 8 7 6 5 4 3 2

Protecting

HUMAN

RIGHTS

WHAT ARE HUMAN RIGHTS AND HOW DO WE PROTECT THEM?

In April 1994, the world watched in amazement as millions of South Africans waited patiently—some in lines more than a half mile long—to vote in a presidential election. Why did people take an election so seriously that they would stand in line for hours to vote? South Africans knew they were making history: It was the first time that citizens of all races were allowed to vote in their country. Voting is an important **human right**—a right that every human being should have.

Voters wait to cast their ballots in South Africa's first democratic election. The election marked the end of apartheid, an official policy of racial segregation and discrimination against black South Africans.

COMMONLY PROTECTED HUMAN RIGHTS

Right to vote
Freedom from slavery
Freedom of thought
Freedom of religion
Right to own property
Freedom of speech
Freedom of the press
Freedom of assembly
Freedom of movement
Right to a fair trial
Right to equal treatment
    before the law

Source: United Nations Declaration
of Human Rights

Journalists in Ukraine hold signs that read
"Censorship Not!" and "Liberty of Speech."
They are peacefully protesting the government's
attempt to force them off radio and television
because they have criticized the government.

THE IMPORTANCE OF HUMAN RIGHTS

The idea of human rights has existed for centuries. Even in ancient Greece, some **philosophers**—people who discuss ideas to gain wisdom—taught that all people have rights that not even kings could take away from them. It was a world-changing idea, but it took almost 2,000 years for governments to begin to respect and protect human rights.

Over time, as democratic institutions developed, the people—not a king or queen—came to be seen as the source of government authority. As a result, some of the earliest laws about human rights safeguarded political rights.

Other commonly protected human rights have been advanced through the years. The trend in recent history has been to grant more human rights around the world. To limit human rights is to limit people's potential. Human rights matter because they preserve the equality and dignity of all people.

KEEPING A WATCHFUL EYE

Although human rights are universal, not all countries protect them, nor do all countries grant exactly the same rights. And even when human rights have been granted, they can be **revoked**, or taken back. This situation can occur when governments are not stable enough to protect human rights, or it may occur when an economic crisis or natural disaster puts pressure on a government. It can happen even in a democracy. For example, in the 1950s, the government of France denied some human rights to people living in Algeria, a North African country that was a French territory at the time.

To prevent such abuses, citizens must work constantly to protect human rights. As you read, you will learn what can happen when people lose human rights and how people around the world have fought to regain them.

Explore the Issue

1. **Summarize** What are human rights, and why are they important?

2. **Draw Conclusions** Which human rights do you think enable people to take part in the political process?

Human Rights

☐ Electoral Democracies

UNITED STATES The U.S. Constitution guarantees the right to vote, but originally that right didn't apply to women and African Americans. African Americans gained voting rights in 1870, and women gained the right in 1920.

LIBYA In 2011, Libyans publicly protested against their leader, Colonel Mu'ammar al-Qadhafi, who had denied basic rights to Libyans. In October, the rebels captured Qadhafi and began a transition to democracy.

CUBA In 2011, the government of Raúl Castro used arrests, beatings, and forced exile to restrict human rights and punish those who criticized the government.

NORTH AMERICA

NORTH ATLANTIC OCEAN

CASE STUDY 1

VENEZUELA President Hugo Chávez has weakened the legislative and judicial branches of government and increased his own power, even going so far as to pass laws on his own.

SOUTH AMERICA

SOUTH PACIFIC OCEAN

SOUTH ATLANTIC OCEAN

Explore the Issue

1. **Find Main Ideas and Details** How does the government of Uzbekistan maintain its control of the country?

2. **Compare and Contrast** Which country has experienced violence associated with elections?

Alert

Study the map below to learn more about human rights situations in countries around the world.

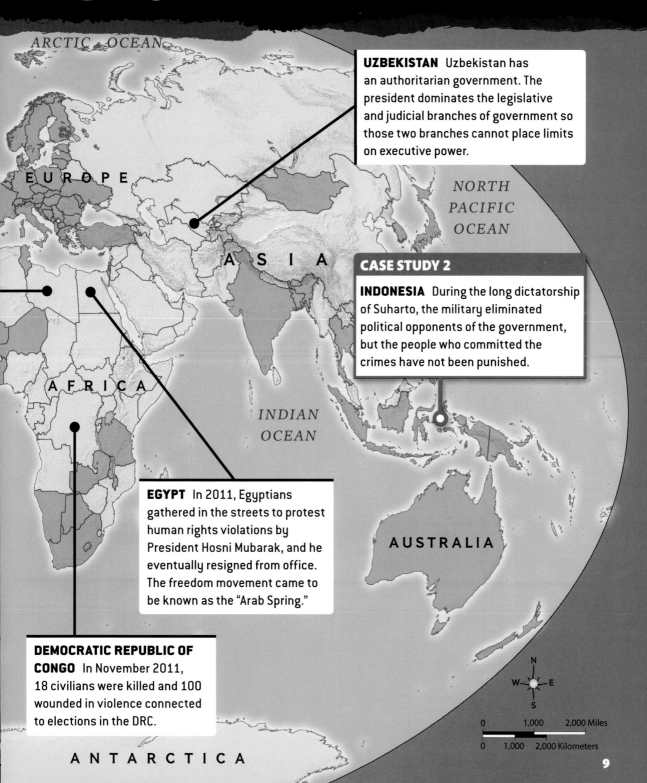

UZBEKISTAN Uzbekistan has an authoritarian government. The president dominates the legislative and judicial branches of government so those two branches cannot place limits on executive power.

ARCTIC OCEAN

EUROPE

NORTH PACIFIC OCEAN

ASIA

CASE STUDY 2

INDONESIA During the long dictatorship of Suharto, the military eliminated political opponents of the government, but the people who committed the crimes have not been punished.

AFRICA

INDIAN OCEAN

EGYPT In 2011, Egyptians gathered in the streets to protest human rights violations by President Hosni Mubarak, and he eventually resigned from office. The freedom movement came to be known as the "Arab Spring."

AUSTRALIA

DEMOCRATIC REPUBLIC OF CONGO In November 2011, 18 civilians were killed and 100 wounded in violence connected to elections in the DRC.

N
W—E
S

0   1,000   2,000 Miles

0   1,000   2,000 Kilometers

ANTARCTICA

SQUASHING DEMOCRACY

in Venezuela

Hundreds of derricks pump oil from Lake Maracaíbo in Venezuela. Oil exports account for a large portion of Venezuela's economy, and Hugo Chávez controls the country's oil-producing industry.

EXERCISING FREEDOM OF SPEECH

Have you ever heard someone claim, "I can say what I want; it's a free country"? In the United States, we take free speech for granted, but in many countries, speaking out can be dangerous. In Venezuela, Oswaldo Alvarez Paz recently learned that lesson.

Alvarez, a member of the political party that opposes Venezuelan president Hugo Chávez, is the former governor of the oil-rich state of Zulia. Many people thought that Alvarez might run for president in the 2012 election. In March 2010, he stated in a television interview that Chávez had allowed Venezuela to become a **haven**, or safe place, for both drug dealers and terrorists. For example, the Venezuelan government was accused of harboring the Revolutionary Armed Forces of Colombia (FARC), a group from neighboring Colombia that is known to raise money from kidnapping and selling illegal drugs. Although many observers outside Venezuela agreed with Alvarez's accusations, the Venezuelan government responded by arresting Alvarez.

GAGGING FREE SPEECH

The government charged Alvarez under a law that prohibits "any individual, by way of print, radio, television, electronic mail, or written leaflets, from using false information to create panic or a sustained anxiety in the general collective." The law means that if a person warns the public that the government is doing something dangerous or illegal, the government can label the accusation "false" and imprison the speaker. Such a system limits free speech. Without free speech, citizens lose one of their strongest weapons against government abuse.

The government claimed Alvarez was urging people to break the law, but international human rights groups believed he was arrested for criticizing Chávez's rule. Critics of Chávez think that Alvarez's real crime was that he spoke the truth. They view Chávez's actions as a serious violation of human rights. According to the United Nations' Universal Declaration of Human Rights, "Everyone has the right to freedom of opinion and expression." Chávez has been accused of violating many of the human rights of Venezuelans. Venezuela's experience demonstrates what happens when a country has one strong ruler.

THE RISE OF CHÁVEZ

To understand why human rights is such a serious issue in Venezuela, it helps to examine the country's recent past. Economic troubles often cause political turmoil. Venezuela's economy depends on exporting oil, and during the 1980s, world oil prices plunged sharply, causing Venezuela's income to drop. The country had more foreign debt than it could repay, so President Carlos Andrés Pérez passed money-raising moves such as increasing bus fares. Riots broke out across the country, and protests continued for two years.

In 1992, a group of army officers led by Chávez tried to overthrow Pérez but failed. Chávez surrendered on the condition that he be allowed to address the nation. In a televised speech, he asked the rebels to lay down their arms "for now." The speech inspired many Venezuelans to view Chávez as a national leader.

He was imprisoned for two years, but then the government dropped all charges against him. In 1998, Venezuelan voters elected Chávez president. Since taking office, he has steered the country toward **socialism**, in which the government owns or controls factories and businesses.

ELIMINATING CHECKS AND BALANCES

Chávez has taken drastic measures to increase his power. He pushed through a new constitution that required new elections of all officials. Chávez was reelected, and his party won a majority in the National Assembly. The legislators appointed pro-Chávez justices to the Supreme Court. Also, the constitution gave Chávez the power to make laws.

In February 2004, President Hugo Chávez salutes the crowd as he gives a speech during a rally in the city of Caracas, the capital of Venezuela.

Because of these changes, Venezuelans have few ways to limit Chávez's power. He does not need the legislature to make laws. The Supreme Court, which decides whether such laws are constitutional, is filled with Chávez supporters.

Chávez has limited the freedoms of speech and the press. International observers have accused him of stealing elections, and in 2009 Chávez had the constitution amended so he can be reelected indefinitely.

President Hugo Chávez of Venezuela delivers a speech to soldiers in October 2011.

During a rally in Caracas, Venezuelan students demand that civil liberties and freedom of expression be upheld. The demonstration was in response to the government shutdown of one of the country's oldest television stations. The word *paz* means "peace" in Spanish.

OTHER VIOLATIONS OF RIGHTS

Even though Chávez himself pushed for the new constitution, his government does not always follow it. On paper, the constitution has strong protections for the rights of indigenous, or native, people, but they are not put into practice. For example, indigenous people have protested coal mining on their lands, claiming that it harms the environment and their lives. Mine operations have damaged water supplies so that they cannot grow crops or raise livestock.

A report issued by the Inter-American Commission on Human Rights (IACHR) in December 2009 listed threats and human rights violations in Venezuela. These include threats to freedom of thought and expression, participation in politics, right to life, personal safety, and liberty.

The IACHR report cited a lack of separation and independence among the branches of government as a serious problem. It also criticized Venezuela for depriving people accused of crimes of fair trials and for terrible prison conditions.

CALLS FOR CHANGE

Human rights activists are concerned about the abuses committed by the Chávez government. They would like to see these changes:

- Return to the **rule of law**—the principle that even the highest government officials must obey the law

- Restoration of separation of powers, which means a strong legislature and court that can limit presidential power

- Protection for human rights, such as freedom of speech, freedom of press, and the right to a fair trial

People around the world are watching Venezuela with concern. Ultimately, however, Venezuelans themselves must restore democracy to their country.

Explore the Issue

1. **Find Main Ideas and Details** What are three ways that the Chávez government has violated human rights?

2. **Make Inferences** How might a strong and independent Supreme Court change Venezuela's situation?

INDONES

From **Dictatorship** to **Democr**

This busy container terminal is located in Jakarta, Indonesia's capital and an important center of trade. In colonial times, Europeans exported spices and other natural resources from the islands. Today, Indonesia's exports include oil, electrical appliances, and textiles.

INDONESIA'S UNIQUE GEOGRAPHY

Indonesia is a difficult country to govern. One reason is its geography: Indonesia is an **archipelago**, or group of islands, that lies between the Pacific and Indian oceans to the southeast of mainland Southeast Asia. The country spans a vast territory extending 3,200 miles from east to west and including 17,000 islands. Because of its location, Indonesia has suffered several natural disasters such as volcanic eruptions and earthquakes that have taken many lives and put enormous strain on the economy at times.

Indonesia's people are as diverse and widespread as the scattered islands, representing a broad variety of **ethnic groups**, or groups that share a cultural origin. Over 580 languages and dialects are spoken in Indonesia (a dialect is a variation of a principal language). For centuries, different groups and individuals have tried to unite this varied country, often through systems that violated the citizens' human rights and caused suffering among Indonesians.

COLONIAL RULE

Europeans began trading in Indonesia in the 1500s. The Moluccas, an island group within the archipelago, were called the Spice Islands by European traders because they were a source of spices such as nutmeg and cloves. These spices were highly prized, and therefore valuable, in Europe. England, the Netherlands, and Portugal all traded in the region and controlled some of the islands at different times. In the 1700s, the Netherlands came to dominate Indonesia through the Dutch East India Company, and in 1815 the Dutch government took direct control over the island country.

Dutch rule was **authoritarian**. That is to say, the Dutch exercised absolute control over Indonesia and its citizens. The Dutch used their superior military power and a **bureaucracy**, or administrative system, to impose their authority and control trade. Dutch government officials at various levels were brought to live in Indonesia and to manage and run the country. Trade between Indonesia and Europe thrived, but very few Indonesian people benefitted. Rather, the standard of living for Indonesians in general declined.

A DICTATOR RISES

In 1942, during World War II, the Dutch lost control of Indonesia when Japan invaded the islands. At first, some Indonesians viewed the Japanese as liberators, freeing the country from Dutch rule, but the Japanese occupation turned out to be equally authoritarian. After Japan was defeated in the war in 1945, an Indonesian man named Sukarno, who had worked for the Japanese, took the reins of government and declared the country's independence.

President Sukarno inspects his troops in 1965.

Sukarno's government was corrupt and ineffective. While proclaiming a goal of national unity, Sukarno lived an extravagant lifestyle, enjoying frequent banquets and other lavish events. He gradually broke apart the country's parliamentary democracy. Sukarno's failures nearly ruined his country's democracy and eventually led to his overthrow.

A SECOND DICTATORSHIP

In 1965 a group of military officers, angered by Sukarno's policies, rebelled and tried to take over the government. The rebellion failed, but it allowed a general named Suharto to gain power. Suharto fought Sukarno for control of the government, and eventually won. Suharto opposed Communism, and in the course of the struggle for power, he led a **purge**, or violent removal, of communists from public life. Thousands were killed.

In 1968, Suharto was elected president of Indonesia, but he proved to be no better than Sukarno when it came to human rights. Indonesia's national legislature went on to elect Suharto seven more times. He never ran in an open election in which citizens choose their leader, but instead used military power to control Indonesian political life and stifle opposition. Suharto's corrupt government allowed relatives and friends to grow wealthy at the country's expense.

During Suharto's rule, many human rights abuses occurred, including arrests of protesters, suppression of the press, mistreatment of prisoners, massacres of communists, and the forcible occupation of the nearby island of East Timor.

Despite arrests and other attempts by the government to eliminate dissent, protests against Suharto did break out. In May 1998, students led a protest demanding that President Suharto resign.

19

Posters along a street in Jakarta advertise local legislative candidates in Indonesia's elections. Indonesia held both parliamentary and presidential elections in 2009.

DEMOCRACY EMERGES

In 1997, an economic crisis gripped the country, but Suharto failed to make reforms. Riots broke out, and the military refused to support Suharto, who resigned in 1998.

Although they caused much suffering, these economic troubles also paved the way for democratic reform. After Suharto resigned, Vice President B. J. Habibie became president and granted amnesty to more than 100 political prisoners, among other actions.

Since Suharto's resignation, Indonesia has had several presidents, including Megawati Sukarnoputri (meh-guh-WAH-tee soo-kar-noh-POO-tree), a daughter of President Sukarno. Megawati worked to improve the economy and resolve conflicts with provinces that had struggled for independence from Indonesia. In 2004, she lost Indonesia's first direct presidential election to Susilo Bambang Yudhoyono (yood-hoh-YOH-noh), who was reelected in 2009.

During Yudhoyono's time in office, Indonesia's economy has improved, and the country has become more stable. Yudhoyono has continued the fight against the corruption that was a hallmark of government under the earlier dictatorships.

Still, many problems remain. The Indonesian government has had to cope with the consequences of natural disasters, for example. In recent years, Indonesia has been hit by tsunamis and volcanic eruptions that killed thousands and forced thousands more from their homes. Disasters such as these can threaten a still-recovering economy.

Indonesia's record on human rights remains imperfect as well. The group Human Rights Watch reports that the military continues to commit abuses in Papua, a province that has tried to separate itself from Indonesia in the past. Indonesia's future as a democracy with protection for human rights looks hopeful, but at this moment it is still a work in progress.

Explore the Issue

1. **Summarize** What human rights abuses have occurred in Indonesia since the Dutch took control?

2. **Draw Conclusions** What can you conclude about the relationship between human rights and political power?

John Bul Dau travels to visit a clinic he helped found in Duk County, South Sudan.

Saving a Lost Generation

Lost Boys and others who have fled Sudan stand in a refugee camp in Kenya.

THE LOST BOYS OF SUDAN

As a boy, National Geographic Emerging Explorer John Bul Dau (BOOL DOW) survived a grueling ordeal. In 1987, during a civil war in Sudan, government troops were sent to attack villages in southern Sudan. Fearing that the government planned to crush the rebellion by killing all southern males, thousands of boys fled to the neighboring country of Ethiopia. Twenty thousand escaping children hiked hundreds of miles through harsh wilderness to get there. Soldiers followed them and tried to capture them. The boys faced other difficulties as well. They did not have enough food to eat or water to drink. They suffered from disease, and many of them died along the way. It was an experience that brutally tested the boys' mental strength as well as their physical endurance.

Thirteen-year-old John Bul Dau was one of those **refugees**, people who have fled their country to escape political danger or natural disaster. Dau's group of refugees are now called the Lost Boys of Sudan. Dau was one of the older boys who helped the younger children survive. "We chewed tall grasses and ate mud to stay alive," he said. "I was barefoot and wearing no clothes; at night the desert was so cold. We thought about our parents all the time."

TORN BY ETHNIC CONFLICT

When Sudan gained independence from Egyptian and British rule in 1956, it had two distinctly different regions. The north held mostly Arab Muslims, and the south held mostly Africans who practiced Christianity or other religions that were common in the region. Independence was granted on the condition that southerners could take part fully in government, but that did not happen. Angry at being excluded, southerners rebelled, starting a war that lasted from 1983 to 2005.

At the time of the Lost Boys' 1987 trek, the fighting was at its worst. Those who made it alive to the bordering country of Ethiopia stayed in refugee camps for several years. In 1991, political turmoil in Ethiopia caused them to flee again, this time to Kenya.

"So many people are still in Sudan needing clinics, schools, and churches. I cannot forget them."—John Dau

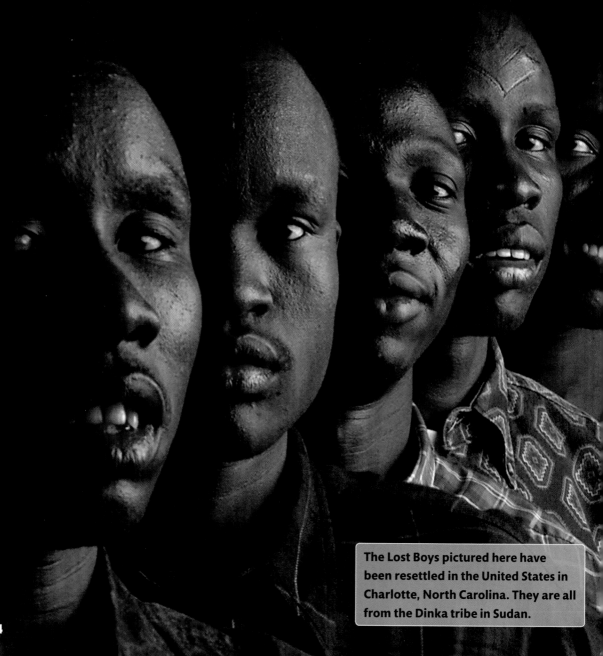

The Lost Boys pictured here have been resettled in the United States in Charlotte, North Carolina. They are all from the Dinka tribe in Sudan.

RELOCATION, RECOVERY, REUNION

Dau was one of the boys who made it to Kenya. At the age of 17, he began his education there, using a stick to scratch letters and numbers in the dirt.

A church in the United States decided to **sponsor**, or be responsible for, several of the Lost Boys and bring them to the United States. Arrangements took some time, and it was 2001 before John Dau reached Syracuse, New York. This young man, who had survived warfare, exile, and starvation, was stunned by the abundance he observed in the United States: "On my first trip to the supermarket I couldn't believe there is an entire aisle of food for cats and dogs."

In 2006, the documentary film *God Grew Tired of Us* told the story of his experience. Dau also continued his education, studying public policy at Syracuse University. Just one year earlier, in 2005, a peace agreement had been signed that finally ended the war in Sudan. Amazingly, 20 years after fleeing from his village, Dau was reunited with his family. Now he encourages others not to give up hope.

MAKING A DIFFERENCE

John Dau believes he made it through his ordeal for a higher purpose. "I feel I survived because God wants to do something with my life. I don't want to waste any of the time I have left. So many people are still in Sudan needing clinics, schools, and churches. I cannot forget them."

To help his people, Dau has set up two **charitable foundations**, organizations that help people. The John Dau Foundation assists refugees, while the South Sudan Institute works for peace, education, and agriculture. Dau also aims to build a health care clinic in South Sudan. John Dau has not forgotten his people—nor his promise to help them.

Explore the Issue

1. **Sequence Events** What were the steps in Dau's journey from Sudan to the United States?

2. **Draw Conclusions** What human rights were violated in this story of the Lost Boys?

Conduct a Survey

Find out which rights the First Amendment of the U.S. Constitution guarantees. Survey people in your community to discover which of these rights people view as most important. For example, ask people if they had to give up one of their rights, which would they choose and why? Make a presentation that describes your survey results and explains the importance of the right that most would give up.

RESEARCH

- Work in pairs as you use the Internet or library to research the First Amendment in the Bill of Rights.

- Write out the full text of the First Amendment. Look up any unfamiliar words you encounter.

- Make a list of protected rights in the First Amendment.

DISCUSS

- Determine the questions you will ask on your survey, and make sure they are worded clearly.

- Decide whether you will survey other students, adults, or a combination of both groups.

- Select a reasonable number of people to survey so that your survey represents the people, or a certain group of people, in your community.

In 2010, citizens in California exercised their right to vote guaranteed by the U.S. Constitution.

ANALYZE

- Examine the data to identify the most important and least important rights based on responses given, and also analyze people's reasons for their choices. Do you notice any patterns?

- Make a graph or chart to organize your data, and be sure to include a title and labels.

- State reasons, facts, and examples to show the importance of the right most would give up.

SHARE

- Make a poster, bulletin, or multimedia presentation to present your results. What conclusions did you draw from your data?

- Conduct a class discussion on this question: Why is it important to protect rights guaranteed by the First Amendment?

- Inspire others to value the First Amendment by discussing instances when these rights have been violated.

Research &
WRITE
Explanatory

Write an
Explanatory Article

When the United States was founded, many states kept African Americans and women from voting. Write an article explaining how the United States gradually changed from that system of government to one of universal suffrage, in which almost all citizens have the right to vote.

RESEARCH

Examine the changes to voting laws that have taken place in the United States since the U.S. Constitution was first adopted. Look for answers to the following questions:

- When was the requirement to own property dropped?
- When and how did women and minorities gain the right to vote? What was the Voting Rights Act of 1965, and why was it important?
- When, how, and why did the voting age change?

Take notes as you research, selecting relevant and well-chosen facts, dates, examples, quotations, and concrete details.

DRAFT

Review your notes, organize your information chronologically, and then write your first draft.

- The introductory paragraph should grab the reader's attention. Preview the ideas that will follow by explaining that the right to vote has spread to new groups over time.
- In the body, explain each event that expanded the right to vote. Use a new paragraph for each event, or summarize all the events in one paragraph that uses appropriate transitions to signal time.
- In the final paragraph, write a conclusion that follows from and supports the information. Be sure to clarify how the expansion of the right to vote relates to human rights and how it affects democracy.

REVISE & EDIT

Read your first draft. Make sure that you have used precise language to explain the events that expanded voting rights since the U.S. Constitution was first adopted.

- Does your attention-getting opening obviously relate to the idea of voting rights?
- Are the ideas in your middle paragraph(s) organized chronologically? Have you clearly explained how each event you cite gave a new group the right to vote?
- Have you used transitions to show the relationship between ideas?
- Does your conclusion link voting to the topics of human rights and democracy?

PUBLISH & PRESENT

Now you are ready to publish and present your article. Print out your article or write a clean copy by hand. Add images, graphs, or time lines to help readers understand the information presented. Post your article in your classroom to share with the class.

Visual GLOSSARY

archipelago *n.*, a group of islands

authoritarian *adj.*, controlling and strict; demanding political obedience

bureaucracy *n.*, the administrative system of a government, made up of officials who are appointed not elected

charitable foundation *n.*, an organization that raises money to help people

ethnic group *n.*, a group of people who share the same cultural background

haven *n.*, a place of safety

human right *n.*, a right that every human being should have

philosopher *n.*, a person who discusses ideas to gain wisdom

purge *n.*, a violent removal of opponents from society

refugee *n.*, a person who has fled a country, usually to escape political danger or a natural disaster

revoke *v.*, to take back

rule of law *n.*, the principle that everyone, even government officials, must obey the law

socialism *n.*, form of government in which the government owns or controls factories and businesses

sponsor *v.*, to support another person financially or make oneself responsible for that person

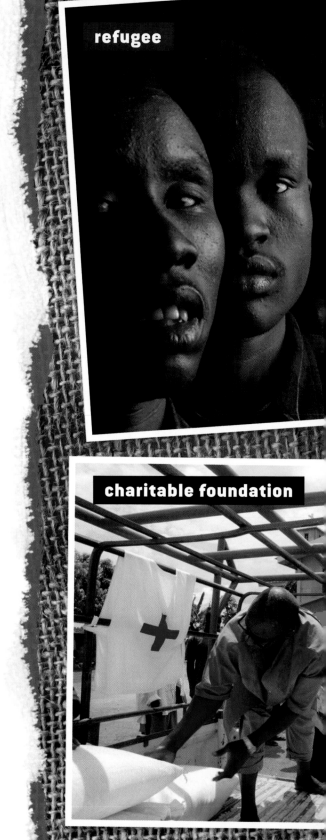

refugee

charitable foundation

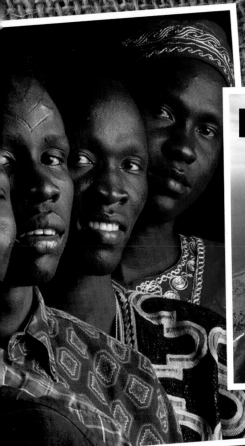

archipelago

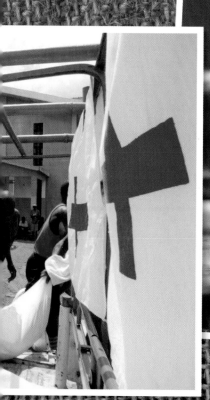

human right

INDEX

SKILLS